DINO DUEL

TRICERATOPS VS. EDMONTOSAURUS

Prehistoric Showdown

Tom Jackson

Lerner Publications ◆ Minneapolis

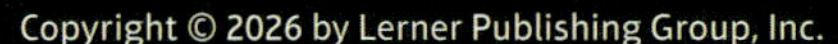

Lerner Publications Company
An imprint of Lerner Publishing Group, Inc.
241 First Avenue North
Minneapolis, MN 55401 USA

For reading levels and more information, look up this title at www.lernerbooks.com.

Main body text set in Aptifer Sans LT Pro.
Typeface provided by Linotype.

Library of Congress Cataloging-in-Publication Data

Names: Jackson, Tom, 1972–author
Title: Triceratops vs. edmontosaurus : prehistoric showdown / Tom Jackson.
Other titles: Triceratops versus edmontosaurus
Description: Minneapolis : Lerner Publications, [2025] | Series: Dino duel | Includes bibliographical references and index. | Audience term: juvenile | Audience: Ages 8–11 Lerner Publications | Audience: Grades 4–6 Lerner Publications | Summary: "Neither the triceratops nor the Edmontosaurus ate meat. But in the fight to survive on scarce resources, these herbivores may have been compelled to fight. Who would win? Read on to find out"—Provided by publisher.
Identifiers: LCCN 2024047150 (print) | LCCN 2024047151 (ebook) | ISBN 9798765669266 (lib. bdg.) | ISBN 9798765683934 (pbk.) | ISBN 9798765676776 (epub)
Subjects: LCSH: Edmontosaurus—Juvenile literature | Triceratops—Juvenile literature
Classification: LCC QE862.O65 J33 2025 (print) | LCC QE862.O65 (ebook) | DDC 567.914—dc23/eng/20250204

LC record available at https://lccn.loc.gov/2024047150
LC ebook record available at https://lccn.loc.gov/2024047151

Manufactured in the United States of America
1 – CG – 7/15/25

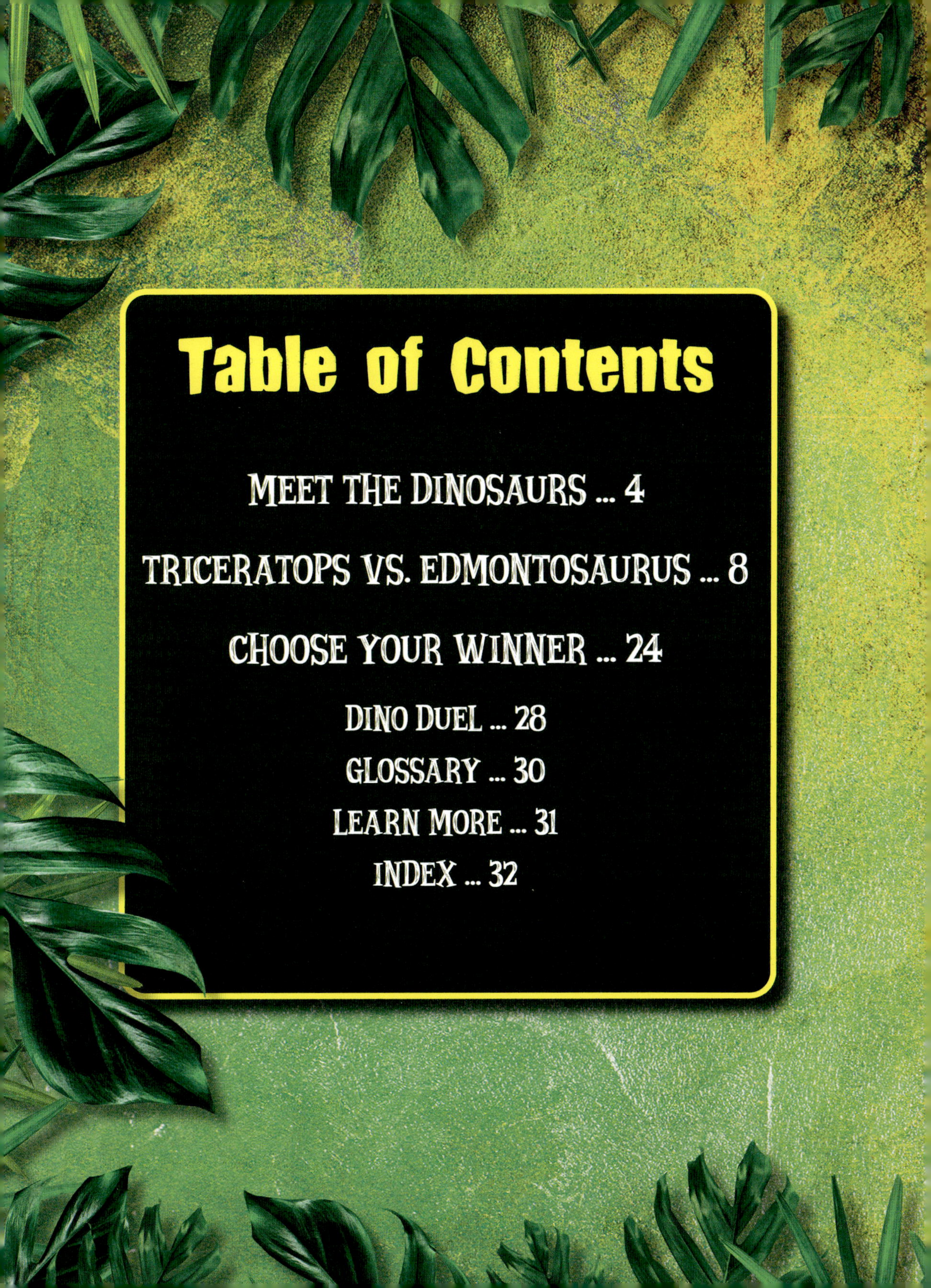

Table of Contents

MEET THE DINOSAURS

Small twigs break under large feet in a quiet forest. A group of Edmontosauruses has stopped at the edge of the forest. They are eating plants and pulling small branches covered in pine needles from the trees. It is cold today, and the breath of the big dinosaurs creates thick clouds in the air.

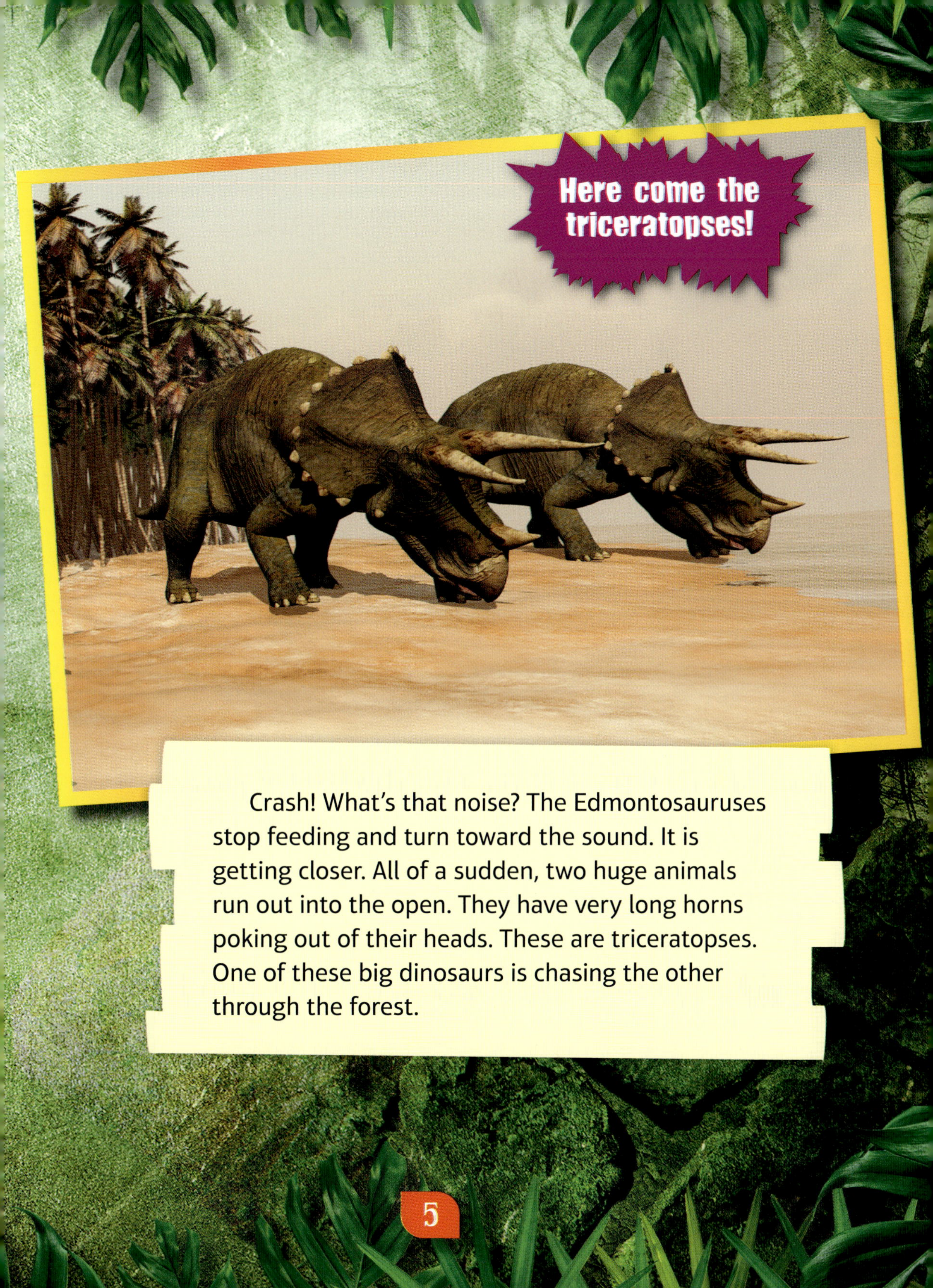

Crash! What's that noise? The Edmontosauruses stop feeding and turn toward the sound. It is getting closer. All of a sudden, two huge animals run out into the open. They have very long horns poking out of their heads. These are triceratopses. One of these big dinosaurs is chasing the other through the forest.

Though the triceratops looked like a fierce predator, it only ate plants.

The triceratopses turn to face each other. They charge and crash their heads and horns together. Both have thick armor on their heads. The smaller triceratops turns away and runs through the herd of Edmontosauruses. He is trying to get away.

The second, larger triceratops starts to chase after him. However, a big Edmontosaurus is in the way. The Edmontosaurus stands up on its back legs. It looks like there is going to be a fight! Who will win?

DINO STATS

Triceratops

Weight: 6.6 tons (6 t)
Length: 26 feet (8 m)
Main weapons: Three sharp horns, bony armor plates

Edmontosaurus

Weight: 6.6 tons (6 t)
Length: 36 feet (11 m)
Main weapons: Large herd, thick skin, fast running speed

TRICERATOPS VS. EDMONTOSAURUS

The skull of an Edmontosaurus

The triceratops and Edmontosaurus lived in what is now North America. They were among the last dinosaurs that died sixty-six million years ago. There were no people around back then. We learn about these two dinosaurs from their fossils. Fossils are bones, teeth, and other body parts that have turned to rock.

There are many fossils of both these dinosaurs. Some of these fossils are of their skin. Skin fossils are very rare. Scientists use fossils to tell how big the dinosaurs were, what they looked like, and how they lived. Both the triceratops and the Edmontosaurus were plant-eaters, but they lived very different lives.

Triceratops skeleton

The name Edmontosaurus means "Lizard from Edmonton." The first of its fossils ever found were near Edmonton, Canada.

Body Size

Both the Edmontosaurus and triceratops were bigger than the animals living today. An Edmontosaurus was about twice as long as an African elephant. The triceratops was not quite as long. However, the triceratops was a very sturdy animal. It looked like a giant version of a rhino.

A relative of the triceratops, called the pentaceratops, had the biggest skull of any land animal in history. The skull was 7 feet 6 inches (2.3 m) long and it would fill a queen size bed!

Both the dinosaurs weighed about the same as four cars. But an Edmontosaurus was longer than a triceratops. Its legs were longer and more slender. The tail of an Edmontosaurus was about the same length as the rest of its body. A triceratops's tail was about half as long as the body.

Speeding Along

Both Edmontosauruses and triceratopses needed to be able to run so they could get away from predators. The biggest predator around at the time was the Tyrannosaurus rex. This hunter had a running speed of about 12 miles (20 km) per hour. A triceratops could manage around 25 miles (40 km) per hour. An Edmontosaurus was even faster. Its top speed was around 28 miles (45 km) per hour.

The Edmontosaurus moved faster thanks to its long legs. A triceratops was very heavy and would get tired quickly when it was running. Triceratopses would only run a short distance to charge at other animals. They did this to drive away attackers and defend their young. Rhinos do the same thing.

Triceratopses were built for fighting. They often attacked each other.

Male triceratopses charged at each other to battle over mates. The winner was normally the animal with the longest horns.

On the Move

Edmontosauruses could switch from walking on their back legs to using all fours. Their long tails helped them keep balance as they stood up. This allowed them to reach high branches. The triceratops always walked on four legs. Its body was too heavy for it to stand up on its back legs.

A triceratops could not lift its head very high. It looked for food near the ground.

Edmontosaurus fossils have been found in northern Alaska. It was much warmer there seventy million years ago, but it still got very dark and cold in the winter.

An Edmontosaurus looks for something to eat.

Edmontosauruses moved long distances every year. In winter, the cold weather would make it harder to find plants to eat. The dinosaurs walked south to where it was warmer. In spring, the dinosaurs headed north again to find fresh food. This kind of animal journey is called a migration. Some Edmontosauruses would cover thousands of miles (km) each year.

Mouth Shapes

Both these dinosaurs had unusual mouths. The triceratops had a hooked beak made of bone. It looked like the mouth of a parrot. The sharp edges of the beak slid past each other as the dinosaur chewed. They worked like a pair of scissors to slice up leaves and twigs.

The Edmontosaurus was a duck-billed dinosaur. It had a wide and flat mouth like a duck. The front of the mouth was made of hard plates of bone. This shape was good for grabbing branches and biting through them.

When the first duck-billed dinosaur fossils were found, early scientists assumed they all lived in water like ducks! More recent experts have figured out that Edmontosauruses did not do this. They could not swim very well.

Feeding Time

Both the Edmontosaurus and the triceratops were plant eaters, but they ate in different ways. The triceratops ate plants that grew near to the ground. It could find food in a forest or in open prairies and meadows. The dinosaur held its head low. That meant its big horns always pointed forward and its mouth was near its food. It plucked some leaves with its beak. It then used its small back teeth to grind the leaves into mush.

Triceratopses often ate grasses and other small plants.

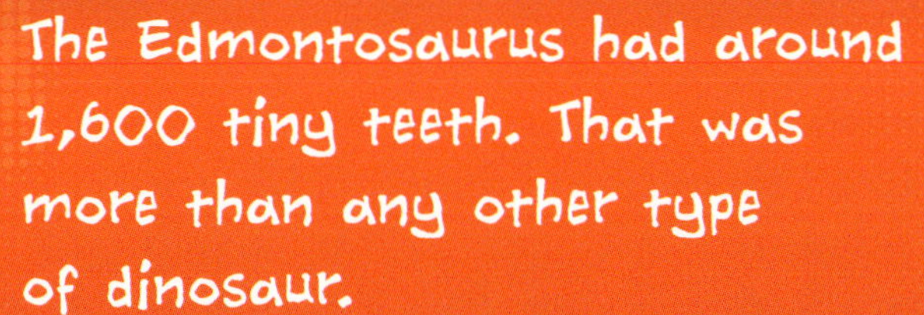

The Edmontosaurus had around 1,600 tiny teeth. That was more than any other type of dinosaur.

The Edmontosaurus traveled long distances to find food.

The Edmontosaurus ate the needles off pine trees. It had to reach up to get this food. Its duckbill mouth curved down a little. This made it easier for an Edmontosaurus to grab a twig and snap it off. In winter, when there was less food around, an Edmontosaurus probably ate tree bark to stay alive.

Living Together

Often the fossil skeletons of Edmontosauruses are found together in groups. This tells scientists that these big animals lived in groups called herds. Being part of a herd would have made the Edmontosauruses safer from attack.

Baby Edmontosauruses stayed close to their mother.

A mother and baby triceratops

No one is sure if triceratopses lived in herds. It is more likely that these dinosaurs stayed with their mothers when they were young. A few fossils have been found with adult and baby skeletons together. However, old triceratopses probably lived alone. They would chase away any other triceratopses that came too close.

A triceratops could defend itself against attack!

Main Weapons

The triceratops was built for fighting. It fought with a sharp bone spike on its snout and two longer spikes above its eyes. There was also a plate of bone at the back of the head. This worked as armor for the neck. Scientists once thought that a triceratops only used these weapons when fighting off attackers like a T. rex. Dinosaur scientists now think the horns and neck plate were also used to show off to other triceratopses and win mates.

The Edmontosaurus was a more gentle creature. Though it was large, it did not have weapons for fighting. Its size made it harder to attack. Skin fossils show that an Edmontosaurus had very thick skin. This was a good defense against bites.

An Edmontosaurus avoided fights. It ran away from danger.

The name *triceratops* means "three-horned face." One relative of the triceratops, the kosmoceratops, had fifteen horns poking out of its face and neck!

CHOOSE YOUR WINNER

The triceratops is not going to stop. It is charging toward the huge Edmontosaurus. Whack! The Edmontosaurus staggers back. The triceratops's horns jabbed the larger dinosaur. It looks like the Edmontosaurus is not hurt thanks to its extra-thick skin.

Now other Edmontosauruses have arrived. They are large adults. They stand in front of the triceratops, making a wall of giant dinosaurs. The younger Edmontosauruses have moved to safety behind their parents. When under attack, this is what many kinds of herd animals do.

The Edmontosaurus had a brain about as big as a baseball. The triceratops's brain was half this size. Their brain was not round, but shaped more like a hot dog.

Now the second, smaller triceratops has come back! It is trying to chase away its bigger rival. If it wins, this male triceratops will be able to breed with any female in the area. Crack! This smaller triceratops hits the other by surprise. That is the winning blow. The larger triceratops runs away.

The fight is over now. The triceratopses and Edmontosauruses are not interested in attacking each other. The winning triceratops takes a bite of some juicy ferns. The herd of Edmontosauruses moves away. They are looking for fresh food. Next time these dinosaurs meet, the fight might end differently.

Some Edmontosaurus fossils had a colorful crest on top of the head. The crest was soft and not made of bone. Scientists think that the strongest Edmontosauruses in the herd had large and bright crests.

Scientists found a fossil horn from a triceratops that shows it was broken by a bite from a T. rex. The horn had healed, which tells us that a triceratops was strong enough to fight off even the toughest dinosaur predators.

DINO DUEL

Triceratops

- Long sharp horns
- Armor plate over the neck
- Heavy and powerful body
- Sharp, beak-shaped mouth

Edmontosaurus

- Huge size
- Fast running speed
- Very thick skin
- Living in herds for safety

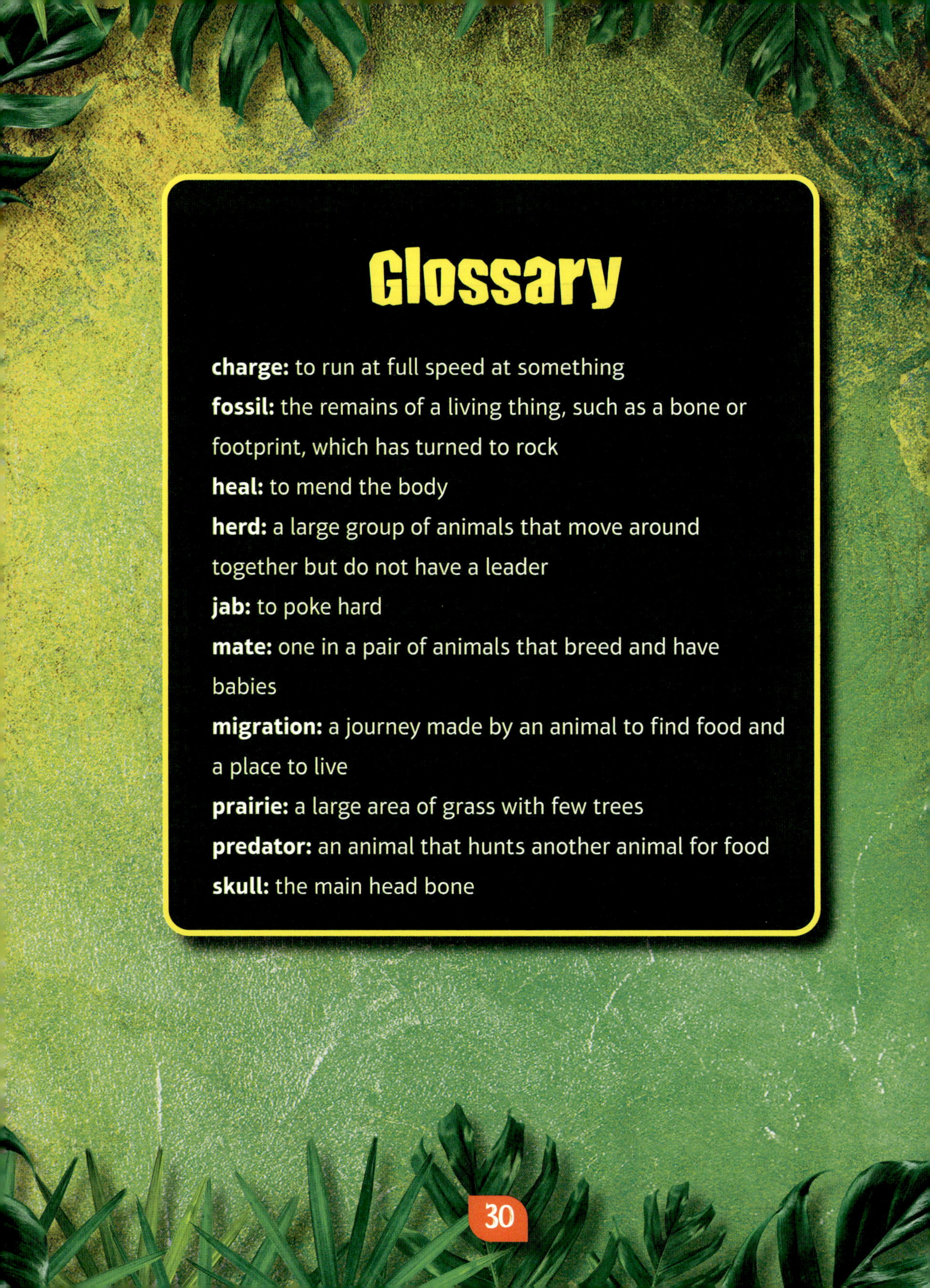

Glossary

charge: to run at full speed at something

fossil: the remains of a living thing, such as a bone or footprint, which has turned to rock

heal: to mend the body

herd: a large group of animals that move around together but do not have a leader

jab: to poke hard

mate: one in a pair of animals that breed and have babies

migration: a journey made by an animal to find food and a place to live

prairie: a large area of grass with few trees

predator: an animal that hunts another animal for food

skull: the main head bone

Learn More

Britannica Kids: Triceratops
https://kids.britannica.com/kids/article/Triceratops/390094

Drimmer, Stephanie Warren. *How to Survive in the Age of Dinosaurs: A Handy Guide to Dodging Deadly Predators, Riding Out Mega-Monsoons, and Escaping Other Perils of the Prehistoric*. Washington, D.C.: National Geographic, 2023.

Jackson, Tom. *T. Rex vs. Ankylosaurus: Prehistoric Showdown*. Minneapolis: Lerner Publications, 2026.

Kiddle: Edmontosaurus Facts for Kids
https://kids.kiddle.co/Edmontosaurus

National Geographic Kids: Triceratops
https://kids.nationalgeographic.com/animals/prehistoric/facts/triceratops

Pallotta, Jerry. *Triceratops vs. Spinosaurus*. New York: Scholastic, 2024.

Index

Photo Acknowledgments

Image credits: Liidia/Shutterstock, p. 1; Catmando/Shutterstock, pp. 4, 20; Corey A Ford/Dreamstime.com, p. 5; Alberto Andrei Rosu/Shutterstock, pp. 6, 13, 24–25; Ton Ponchai/Shutterstock, pp. 7a, 11; Drumheller S. K., Boyd C. A., Barnes B. M. S., Householder M. L./Wikimedia Commons, p. 7b; Nancy Kaszerman/ZUMA Press Wire/Shutterstock, p. 8; Barks/Shutterstock, p. 9; Unexpecteddinolesson/Wikimedia Commons, p. 10; Lerner Vadim/Shutterstock, p. 12; Orla/Shutterstock, p. 14; Wolfhound911/Dreamstime.com, pp. 15, 23, 24; Vladimir Bolokh/Shutterstock, pp. 16, 22; Volodymyr Muliar/Dreamstime.com, p. 17; Herschel Hoffmeyer/Shutterstock, p. 18; Daniel Eskridge/Shutterstock, p. 19; Dotted Yeti/Shutterstock, p. 21; Malchev/Dreamtime.com, p. 27; Vasyl Hedzun/Shutterstock, p. 28; Warpaint/Shutterstock, p. 29. Design elements: Kompaniets Taras/Shutterstock; Chaiyapong/Shutterstock.

Cover: Liidia/Shutterstock; Kompaniets Taras/Shutterstock; Chaiyapong/Shutterstock; Vladimir Bolokh/Shutterstock (top); Simon Bennett/Shutterstock (bottom); Wolfhound911/Dreamstime.com .